Would You Rather?

Game Book
For
Kids and Family

200 Funny Scenarios, Wacky Choices
and Hilarious Situations for
the Whole Family

*With Fun
Illustrations*

RIDDLELAND

Table of Contents

Special Bonus

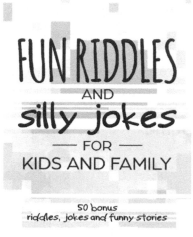

FUN RIDDLES
AND
silly jokes
— FOR —
KIDS AND FAMILY

50 bonus
riddles, jokes and funny stories

RIDDLELAND

SCAN ME

https://pixelfy.me/riddlelandbonus

Thank you for buying this book. We would like to share a special bonus as a token of our appreciation. It is a collection of 50 original jokes, riddles, and two super funny stories!

Introduction

"The QUESTION is the primary form of communication for little kids" – Jim Gaffigan

We would like to personally thank you for purchasing this book. **Would you rather game book for kids and family** is a collection of 200 of the funniest scenarios, wacky choices, and hilarious situations for kids and adults to choose from. It is also filled with fun and cute illustrations.

These questions are an excellent way to get a conversation started in a fun and exciting way. Also, by asking "Why?" after a "would you rather question," you may find interesting answers and learn a lot about a person.

We wrote this book because we want children to be encouraged to read more, think, and grow. As parents, we know that when children play games and learn, they are being educated while having so much fun that they don't even realize they're learning and developing valuable life skills. 'Would you Rather ...' is one of our favorite games to play as a family. Some of the 'would you rather ...' scenarios have had us in fits of giggles, others have generated reactions such as: "eeeeeeuuugh that's gross!" and yet others still really make us think and reflect and consider our decisions.

Besides having fun, playing the game also has other benefits such as:

- **Communication** – This game helps children to interact, read aloud, and listen to others. It's a great way to connect. It's a fun way for parents to get their children interacting with them without a formal, awkward conversation. The game can also help to get to know someone better and learn about their likes, dislikes, and values.

- **Builds Confidence** - Children get used to pronouncing vocabulary, asking questions and it helps to deal with shyness.

- **Develops Critical Thinking** – It helps children to defend and justify the rationale for their choices and can generate discussions and debates. Parents playing this game with young children can give them prompting questions about their answers to help them reach logical and sensible decisions.

- **Improves Vocabulary** – Children will be introduced to new words in the questions, and the context of them will help them remember them because the game is fun.

- **Encourages Equality and Diversity** – Considering other people's answers, even if they differ from your own, is important for respect, equality, diversity, tolerance, acceptance, and inclusivity. Some questions may get children to think about options available to them, that don't fall into gendered stereotypes, i.e., careers or activities that challenge the norm.

Rules of the Games

This game is probably best played with other people, so if you can, play it with friends or family.

If you have two players

- Player one takes the book and asks the player two a question beginning with the phrase, "Would you rather...? "Why?"

- After player 2 has made his/her choice, he/she has to explain the reason why the choice was made.

- Pass the book to the other player, and they ask you a question.

- Learn lots about one another, have fun and giggles.

- The two-player game version could work well as an ice-breaker exercise before introductions in classes or meetings.

If you have three or four players

- Out of your group, decide who will be the Question Master. If you can't decide, have folded bits of paper with 'Question Master' written on one, and 'players' on the other and each pick one.

- The Question Master asks one question from the book.

- The other two or three people give their answers.

- The Question Master decides who has given the best answer – this is the answer with the best explanation for why. The explanations can be funny or creative or well thought out. The Question Master's decision is final. One point is given for the best answer. If the Question Master can't decide, both players get one point each.

- The first player to reach a score of 10 points wins.

Let The Fun Begin!

Eat a pineapple
or
a strawberry that is rotten?

Always win every game you play
or
find 10 dollars every time you
clean your room?

Would You Rather...

Not get to watch TV
or
not use an iPad for 30 days?

Sail on a ship made of gummy
bears
or
chocolate bark?

★ ★ ★ Would You Rather... ★ ★ ★

Ride in a big tank
or
fly in a helicopter?

Have the scales of an armadillo
or
tough skin like a honey badger?

Would You Rather...

Live in a cabin in the forest
or
live in an igloo in the North Pole?

Win a Nobel prize
or
a 10-million-dollar lottery?

Would You Rather...

Ride on an ostrich
or
a rhinoceros?

Have excellent drawing skills but
terrible handwriting
or
excellent handwriting but terrible
drawing skills?

Would You Rather...

Have long arms like a monkey
or
sharp spikes like a porcupine?

Be surrounded by ten babies
or
stuck on an island by yourself for
one whole year?

★ ★ ★ **Would You Rather...** ★ ★ ★

Ride in a horse and carriage
or
on a unicycle?

Not be able to talk
or
be blind for the next five years
of your life?

Would You Rather...

Have a kangaroo
or
a koala bear as a pet?

Save a person's life today
or
save ten lives over three years?

Would You Rather...

Have a dog that meows
or
a cat that barks?

Live without music
or
live without movies for your
entire childhood?

Would You Rather...

Eat cold food
or
eat hot food for the rest of your
life?

Sail around the world
or
drive and fly around the world?

⭐ ⭐ ⭐ **Would You Rather...** ⭐ ⭐ ⭐

Eat a big bowl of mayonnaise
or
drink a cup of olive oil?

Have to yodel
or
have to beatbox every time you
open a door?

★ ★ ★ Would You Rather... ★ ★ ★

Live in a house made of pudding
or
a house made of marshmallow?

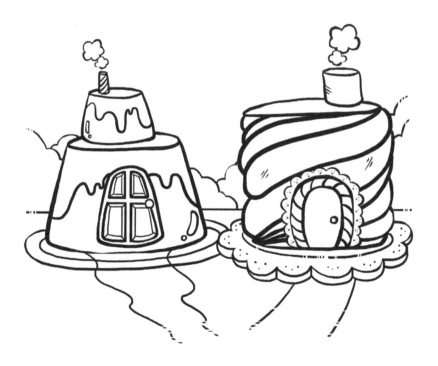

Have one year of winter and
then five months of summer
or
two years of winter and one year
of summer?

Would You Rather...

Have a personal robot assistant
or
a pet dog that can talk?

Be an actor or actress in a real
movie
or
be an animated character?

Be a great singer
or
a great dancer?

Have a tough life for the first 20
years and then an easy life
or
have an easy life for the first 30
years and then a normal plain
life?

Would You Rather...

Have everything smell like roses
or
have everything taste like
cheese?

Be very smart but poor
or
be very wealthy but naïve?

Would You Rather...

Have pizza
or
have pasta for breakfast every
morning?

Be unhealthy but live until you
are 100 years old
or
be healthy but only live until you
are 60 years old?

Would You Rather...

Lick your shoes
or
pick your nose?

Have a million dollars
or
a penny that doubles every day
for 30 days?

Be very flexible like a gymnast
or
be very strong like a wrestler?

Be your own boss
or
work as an assistant for a
multimillionaire?

Would You Rather...

Eat only ice cream
or
eat only chocolate for the rest
of your life?

Live next to an active volcano
or
live next to a swamp full of
alligators?

Be friends with Wonder Woman
or
Aqua man?

Be a famous patisserie chef
or
be a famous baker?

★ ★ ★ Would You Rather... ★ ★ ★

Eat only green beans
or
eat only broccoli for an entire
year?

Live in a small hut by the beach
or
live in a tent on top of a
mountain?

★ ★ ★ **Would You Rather...** ★ ★ ★

Turn into a unicorn
or
become a centaur every 1st day
of the month?

Be the most popular kid in town
or
be the teacher's pet?

Would You Rather...

Have strong front teeth like a
beaver
or
have large fangs like a
sabertooth tiger?

Always be 1 hour early
or
always be 2 minutes late?

Would You Rather...

Be able to go through walls
or
become indestructible?

See a minute of your future
or
see a minute of your friend's
future?

★ ★ ★ **Would You Rather...** ★ ★ ★

Wash your hair once a month
or
brush your teeth once a week?

Be terrible at cooking
or
terrible at baking?

Would You Rather...

Ride a train to school
or
travel in a hot air balloon to
school every day?

Wake up early
or
go to bed late?

Would You Rather...

Be able to teleport from one
place to another
or
run lightning-fast like the Flash?

Eat uncooked bread dough
or
eat uncooked cake batter?

Have no money and feel happy
or
have a lot of money and feel
miserable?

Be able to get away with any lie
or
be able to tell if someone is
lying?

Would You Rather...

Be able to turn into a dragon
or
able to turn into a phoenix?

Skip school every day
or
get to watch as much television
as you want after school every
day?

Would You Rather...

Learn how to bake bread
or
how to bake sweet treats like
cakes
and donuts?

Create a new cartoon show
or
create a new holiday?

Have a panda
or
a hippo as a pet?

Have a photographic memory
or
be able to speed read multiple
books at a time?

★ ★ ★ Would You Rather... ★ ★ ★

Be a world-famous detective
or
a famous spy?

Be able to do cartwheels
or
front and backflips?

Would You Rather...

Slide down a big water slide
or
go zip lining?

Write a new book
or
create a new movie?

Go wakeboarding
or
parasailing?

Live in a virtual reality world
where everything is perfect
or
live in a reality where things
are up and down?

Would You Rather...

Wear the same clothes for seven days
or
drink spoiled milk?

Own a McDonalds franchise
or
a Pizza Hut franchise?

Be a snail
or
a beetle?

Be stuck inside a lift
or
a ski lift for 2 days?

Would You Rather...

Exercise when it is very hot
or
when it is freezing cold?

Lose the ability to read
or
lose the ability to listen to
music?

Would You Rather...

Eat broccoli
or
eat spinach for every meal?

Be able to speak any language
or
be able to understand animals?

Would You Rather...

Have a personal chef that cooks
all your favourite meals
or
a personal butler that manages
your daily schedule?

Never be able to speak again
or
have to say everything you think
out loud?

★ ★ ★ Would You Rather... ★ ★ ★

Be able to draw any imaginary
thing and make it come alive
or
be able to make any real thing
disappear by erasing it?

Live an extra 50 years
or
be given $5,000,000 and only
live until 80 years old?

★ ★ ★ Would You Rather... ★ ★ ★

Wear wet shirts
or
wet socks for a whole month?

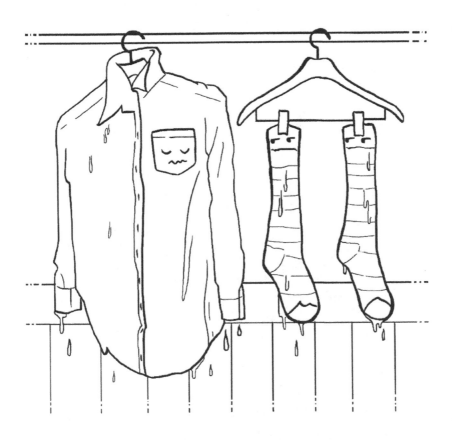

Have more good friends
or
be successful at work?

★ ★ ★ Would You Rather... ★ ★ ★

Live in ancient Egypt as a
Pharaoh
or
in ancient England as a King?

Travel anywhere for free for the
rest of your life
or
have a house for free anywhere
in the world?

Only eat chicken and waffles
or
blueberry pancakes with bacon
for dinner every night?

End world hunger
or
have world peace?

★ ★ ★ Would You Rather... ★ ★ ★

Be turned into a werewolf
or
turned into a vampire?

Always have hiccups
or
always feel like you need to
sneeze but can't?

Would You Rather...

Sit and do nothing every day
or
eat the same food every day for
the rest of your life?

Only be able to say Hee-haw
like a donkey when someone
is telling a joke
or
only be able to laugh and
snort like a pig when someone
is telling bad news?

Be a circus acrobat
or
be a magician?

Be able to relive your life and
correct your mistakes
or
live to 100 years old?

Would You Rather...

Have six legs
or
six arms?

Be the bad hero
or
the good villain in a movie?

Turn into a dwarf
or
become an ogre once one week?

Be able to talk to your pet
or
have your pet live for as long as
you?

Would You Rather...

Dance in the rain
or
in the snow?

Never have to sleep
or
never have to use the restroom?

Would You Rather...

Always wake up with perfect hair
or
only need to shower once a
week?

Never have to eat to survive
or
always be able to remember
your dreams?

Would You Rather...

Have hair all over your body like
an Orang-Utan
or
be hairless like a Siamese cat?

Be a doctor that saves lives
every day
or
a famous politician?

Be very good at all computer
games
or
excel at board games?

Be able to stop time for 5
minutes
or
rewind time for 2 minutes?

Would You Rather...

Be as tall as a giant
or
as small as a hobbit?

Be able to shape shift to any
animal
or
mind control animals, up to 50
meters away?

Never feel sad again
or
never feel angry again?

Always tell the truth
or
sometimes tell a white lie so
long as people don't get hurt?

Would You Rather...

Eat French fries with ice cream
or
consume cheese dipped in hot
chocolate?

Have cold showers every
morning
or
sleep 2 hours less than your
usual amount?

Be stranded on an island full of
cheese
or
stranded on an island full of
bacon?

Live in the same city for the rest
of your life
or
have to move to a new location
every four months?

Would You Rather...

Have a magic cup that is always
filled with your favourite soda
or
have a magic plate that is
always filled your favourite dish?

Be able to copy any dance move
after seeing it once
or
be able to imitate any voice after
hearing it once?

Would You Rather...

Be a ninja
or
a space cowboy?

Stay in school until you are
30 years old
or
not be able to leave your home
for five years?

Would You Rather...

Have infinite power
or
infinite knowledge?

Drink a glass of milkshake made
with green olives
or
drink a glass of seawater?

★ ★ ★ Would You Rather... ★ ★ ★

Own a monster truck
or
own a chariot with a horse?

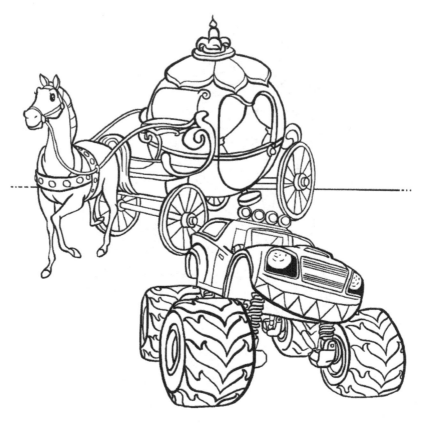

Be trapped in a room full of
tarantula spiders
or
spend a night in the cemetery?

⭐ ⭐ ⭐ **Would You Rather...** ⭐ ⭐ ⭐

Spend a decade under the sea
in a submarine
or
a decade in space in a
spaceship?

Have smelly feet
or
super long fingernails?

★ ★ ★ Would You Rather... ★ ★ ★

Visit Narnia
or
Hogwarts?

Have your parents become your
age
or
you become your parents' age?

Wrestle with a gorilla
or
wrestle a honey bear?

Be able to remember everything
from the day you were born
or
learn about how you will die?

Would You Rather...

Be stuck at sea on a raft
or
be stuck at sea in a canoe?

Be the King of a country
or
start your own colony on Mars?

Would You Rather...

Live on an island made of pizza
or on an island made of mac
and cheese?

Be able to stare at people for
hours without blinking
or
be able to sneeze without
closing your eyes?

★ ★ ★ Would You Rather... ★ ★ ★

Wear summer clothes during
winter
or
winter clothes during the
summer?

Wear the same shirt for one
month
or
not take off your shoes for one
month?

★ ★ ★ Would You Rather... ★ ★ ★

Live on a peaceful island by
yourself
or
live in a dangerous city with
your family?

Have your birthday as a national
holiday
or
have a city named after you?

★ ★ ★ Would You Rather... ★ ★ ★

Have a lightsabre
or
have a Cloak of Invisibility?

Have perfect hair when you
wake up
or
never have to wash your face
every morning?

Would You Rather...

Be able to breathe underwater
or
breathe in space without special
apparatus?

Never go hungry
or
never go thirsty for the rest
of your life?

Be the only child
or
have six siblings?

Be the luckiest person in the
world
or
share your luck with your
family and friends?

Would You Rather...

Jump into a lake
or
play in a pigsty?

Eat a fried grilled cheese
sandwich
or
eat a fried oreo?

★ ★ ★ **Would You Rather...** ★ ★ ★

Have to wear funny hats
or
wear funny shoes every day?

Have a backpack that can
transform into any car you want
or
a plate that can make any food
you want?

Be a secret spy with cool
gadgets
or
a mad scientist with cool
inventions?

Fight with a lion-sized rhinoceros
beetle
or
fight ten dog-sized tarantula
spiders?

★ ★ ★ Would You Rather... ★ ★ ★

Be friends with the Easter Bunny
or
the Tooth Fairy?

Listen to a movie without the
video
or
watch a movie without sound or
subtitles?

Would You Rather...

Eat hot dogs
or
burgers for the entire year?

Be able to make one wish come
true for yourself
or
make ten wishes come true for
other people?

Be a Viking
or
a caveman?

Have six spider legs
or
eight octopus tentacles?

Travel through space on a
surfboard
or
travel through time on a
skateboard?

Have the power to control other
people's dreams
or
the power to control your own
dreams?

★ ★ ★ Would You Rather... ★ ★ ★

Walk upside down on your hands
or
walk on all fours using your arms
and legs?

Have the face of a baboon
or
the butt of a baboon?

Would You Rather...

Turn into an elf
or
turn into a fairy?

Wake up with a different
hairstyle
or
be a different height every
morning?

★ ★ ★ Would You Rather... ★ ★ ★

Be able to walk up the sides of buildings
or
be able to jump over a building?

Be transported to 100 years in the future
or
transported to 1 year in the past?

Would You Rather...

Ride on a Griffin
or
ride on a Pegasus?

Have a remote control that can
pause, fast forward or rewind a
person's life
or
have the power to control a
person's actions?

Would You Rather...

Have a llama
or
a narwhal as a pet?

Be a math whiz
or
fluent in a foreign language?

★ ★ ★ Would You Rather... ★ ★ ★

Be able to stop the rain every
time you sneeze
or
make a thunderstorm when
you're angry?

Have a big body
or
a very small head?

Would You Rather...

Learn how to sculpt a statue
or
learn how to create pottery?

Create a new dish
or
make a classic dish disappear?

Would You Rather...

Go dog sledding
or
go sandboarding?

Be able to recharge your body
through solar power
or
recharge your body through
eating canned spinach?

★ ★ ★ Would You Rather... ★ ★ ★

Go water skiing
or
go zorbing?

Live on an island that has a
volcano that can erupt at any time
or
live in a city that has an
earthquake every week?

Would You Rather...

Be chased by a swarm of
mosquitoes
or
be chased by a swarm of bees?

Eat any food you want
or
go to bed at any time you want?

Would You Rather...

Eat a whole watermelon
or
eat a whole cantaloupe?

Smile every time you are sad
or
cry every time you are happy?

Would You Rather...

Have a cat that is also a butler
or
have a dog that is also a butler?

Be able to see in the dark
or
swim with your eyes open?

Turn into a Dracula
or
turn into Frankenstein's
monster?

Hear everything 5 minutes late
or
be almost deaf?

Would You Rather...

Eat only fruit for a week
or
eat only meat for a week?

Yawn when you are energetic
or
giggle when you are sleepy?

Would You Rather...

Eat frozen peas
or
frozen turnips?

Eat a can of worms
or
eat a can of crickets?

Would You Rather...

Have a platypus
or
an otter as a pet?

Watch YouTube
or
Netflix for an entire day?

Would You Rather...

Be a ventriloquist
or
be a magician?

Live in the world of Harry Potter
or
live in the world of Star Wars?

Would You Rather...

Have large moose antlers
or
long Texas bull horns?

Be allergic to sugar
or
be allergic to television?

Would You Rather...

Be able to heal any wound by
blowing on it
or
teleport every time you burp?

Have to hunt for everything
you eat
or
eat only raw carrots for
every meal?

Would You Rather...

Kiss a snake
or
a jellyfish?

Always be respected
or
have unlimited power?

Be abducted by aliens
or
be abducted by sea monsters?

Live in your current house
or
live in your dream house without
the internet?

Would You Rather...

Go air gliding
or
bungee jumping?

Be the worst player on a sports
team that always wins
or
the best player on a sports team
that always loses?

Would You Rather...

Be the Captain of a navy ship
or
a General for an army?

Live in the Pokemon Universe
or
the Marvel Superheroes
Universe?

One Final Thing...

Thank for making it through to the end of **Would You Rather?,**
Game Book for Kids and family, let's hope it was fun, silly and
able to provide you and your family with all of the entertainment
you needed for this rainy day (or sunny afternoon)!

Did you enjoy the book?

If you did, please let us know by leaving a review on AMAZON.
Reviews let Amazon know that we are creating quality material
for children. Even a few words and ratings would go a long way.
We would like to thank you in advance for your time.

If you have any comments, or suggestions for improvement for
other books, we would love to hear from you, and you can
contact us at **riddleland@riddlelandforkids.com**
Your comments are greatly valued, and the book has already
been revised and improved as a result of helpful suggestions
from readers.

Other Fun Children Books for Kids!

Riddles Series

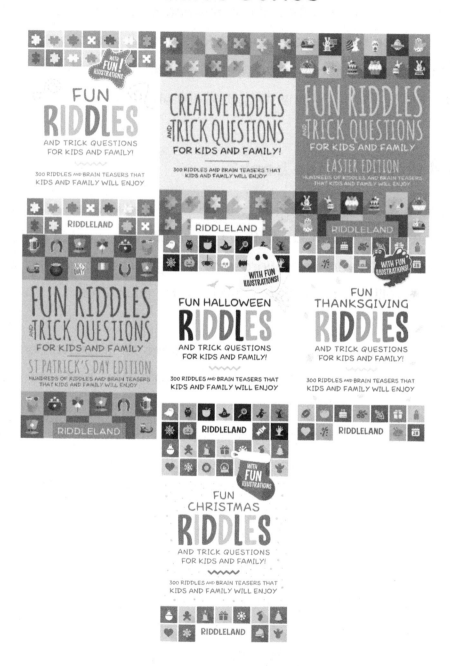

The Laugh Challenge Series

Would You Rather? Books

Get them on Amazon

or our website at www.riddlelandforkids.com

Special Bonus

RIDDLELAND

https://pixelfy.me/riddlelandbonus

Thank you for buying this book. We would like to share a special bonus as a token of our appreciation. It is a collection of 50 original jokes, riddles, and two super funny stories!

RIDDLE AND JOKE CONTESTS!!

Riddleland has two contests to see who are the smartest or funniest boys and girls in the world:
1) **Creative and Challenging Riddles**
2) **Tickle Your Funny Bone Contest**

Parents, please email us your child's "original" riddle or joke and **he or she could win a $25 Amazon gift card.**

Here are the rules:
1) It must be challenging for the riddles and funny for the jokes!
2) It must be 100% original and not something from the Internet! It is easy to find out!
3) You can submit both jokes and riddles as they are 2 separate contests.
4) No help from the parents unless they are as funny as you.
5) Winners will be announced via email.
6) Please also mention what book you purchased.
7) Email us at Riddleland@riddlelandforkids.com

About Riddleland

Riddleland is a mom + dad run publishing company. We are passionate about creating fun and innovative books to help children develop their reading skills and fall in love with reading. If you have suggestions for us or want to work with us, shoot us an email at riddleland@riddlelandforkids.com

Our favourite family quote:

"**Creativity is an area in which younger people have a tremendous advantage since they have an endearing habit of always questioning past wisdom and authority.**" – **Bill Hewlett**

Made in the USA
Monee, IL
10 December 2020